Victoria

Romantic Touches

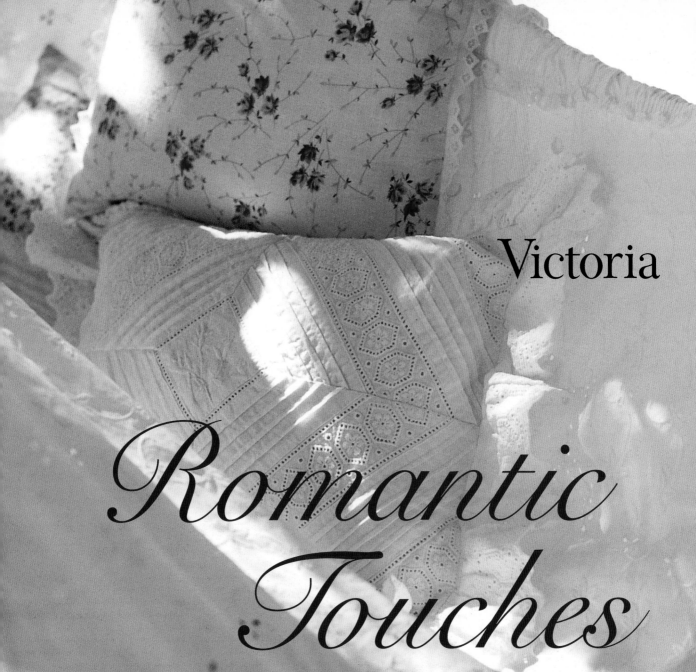

Victoria

Romantic Touches

Charming Handmade Projects for Every Room

GILLIAN HASLAM

HEARST BOOKS
A Division of Sterling Publishing Co., Inc.
New York

Copyright © 2004 by Hearst Communications, Inc.

This book was previously published as a hardcover.

Designed by Christine Wood
Illustrations by Kate Simunek

Photo Credits:
Front cover by Christophe Dugied
Back cover (left to right) by Toshi Otsuki, Toshi Otsuki, Christophe Dugied
Spine by Christophe Dugied

Library of Congress Cataloging-in-Publication Data
Available upon request.

10 9 8 7 6 5 4 3 2 1

First Paperback Edition 2006
Published by Hearst Books
A Division of Sterling Publishing Co., Inc.
387 Park Avenue South, New York, NY 10016

Hearst Books is proud to continue the superb style, quality, and tradition of *Victoria* magazine with every book we publish. On our beautifully illustrated pages you will always find inspiration and ideas about the subjects you love.

Victoria and Hearst Books are trademarks of Hearst Communications, Inc.

For information about custom editions, special sales, premium and corporate purchases, please contact Sterling Special Sales Department at 800-805-5489 or specialsales@sterlingpub.com.

Distributed in Canada by Sterling Publishing
c/o Canadian Manda Group, 165 Dufferin Street
Toronto, Ontario, Canada M6K 3H6

Distributed in Australia by Capricorn Link (Australia) Pty. Ltd.
P.O. Box 704, Windsor, NSW 2756 Australia

Manufactured in China

Sterling ISBN 13: 978-1-58816-617-3
ISBN 10: 1-58816-617-1

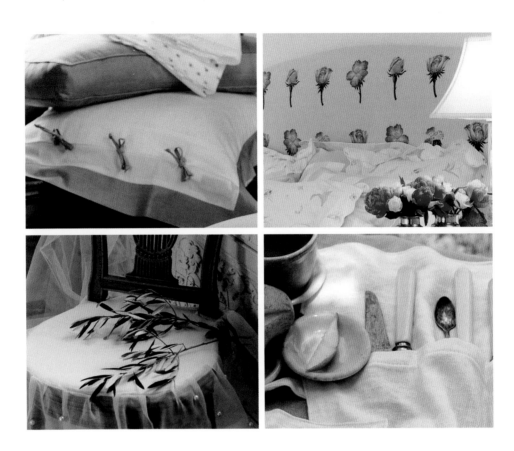

contents

introduction

Turning a house into a home is all about personalizing it, about moving away from the uniformity of mass-produced home furnishings and styling the rooms with special touches to reflect your individuality.

In this book, we have gathered together a stylish collection of projects to help you add your own touch to the living room, the bedroom, and the dining room. All the projects are easy to sew and many only require the simplest of skills—if you can stitch a straight seam, then you can manage these ideas. Many of the projects just use a small amount of fabric, so you can change the look of a room simply by adding a few new pillows or a seat cover. And if you're not inclined to make the projects completely from scratch, you can even use some of the design ideas to embellish ready-made furnishings, such as decorating a store-bought pillow cover or trimming a plain headboard with bands of colored silky ribbons.

Whether you want to turn plain kitchen chairs into something special, bring a touch of sheer luxury to your bedroom, dress your windows with stylish drapes, update your sofa with the classiest of pillows, make scented sachets for your closet, or add glamour to your dining table, you will find the perfect solution in this book.

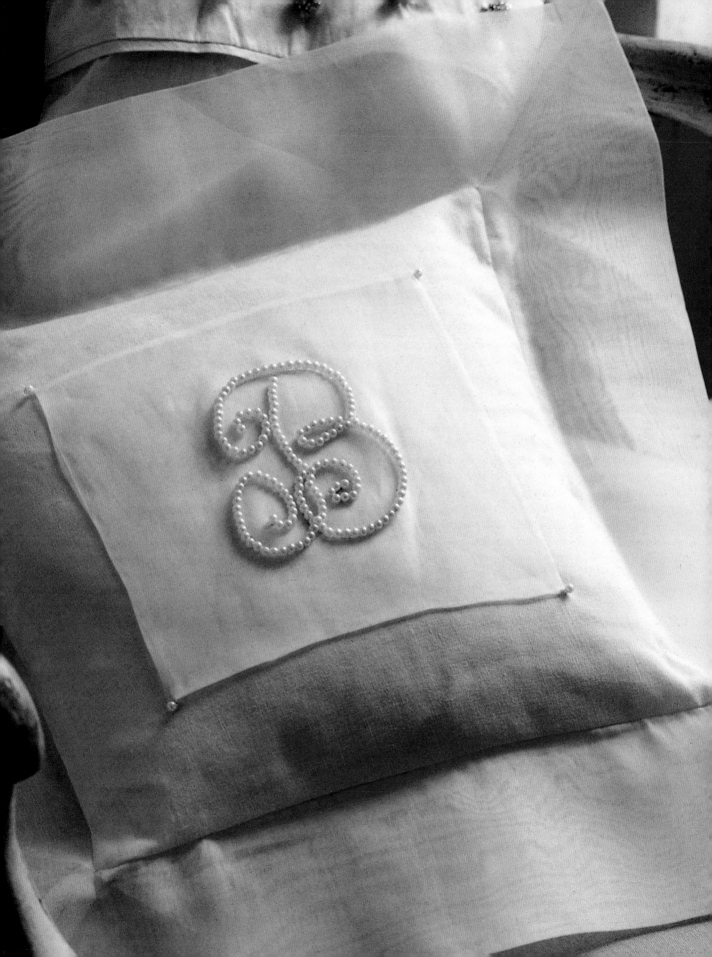

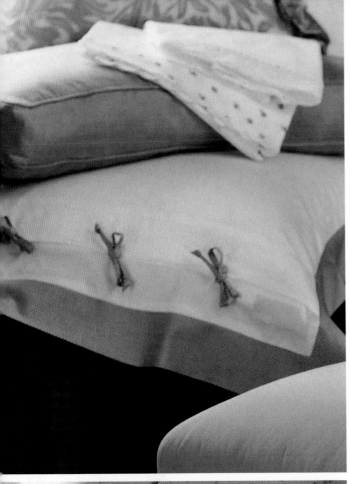

chapter one

pillows and curtains

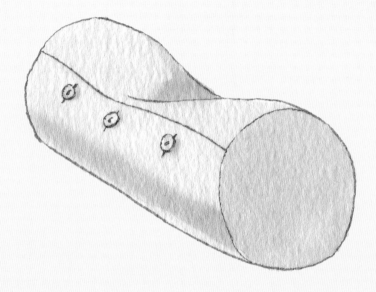

cream bolster pillow

This comfortingly plump bolster pillow is made from unbleached muslin and provides the perfect foil for the bright pinks, yellows, and oranges of the pillows it accompanies. When using bright colors such as these, it's a good idea to add a few touches of cool, solid-color fabrics to provide contrast and to prevent the rich color scheme from becoming overwhelming. The rounded shape of this bolster complements the pleasing curves of the chair and footstool.

YOU WILL NEED

Unbleached muslin

Bolster pillow form

Tape measure

Scissors

Pins

Sewing machine, with buttonhole attachment

Needle and thread

Three large cream buttons

TIP

Rather than using plain buttons, you could cover buttons to match the fabric. Simply buy a button-covering kit, available from most fabric or craft stores.

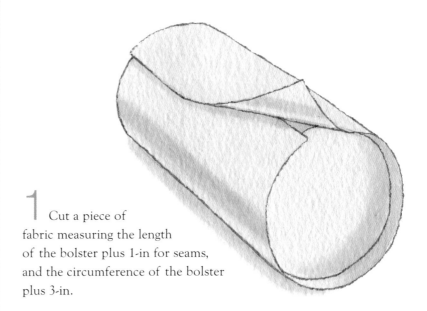

1 Cut a piece of fabric measuring the length of the bolster plus 1-in for seams, and the circumference of the bolster plus 3-in.

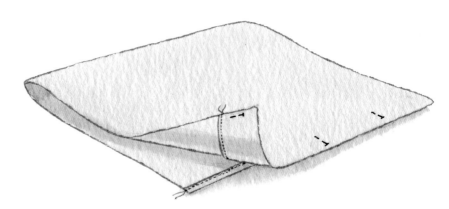

2 Fold, pin, press, and stitch a ½-in hem along the two sides of the bolster fabric. Turn one of the hemmed edges over by 2-in, wrong sides facing, and pin together. Mark the position of the three buttonholes with pins. Stitch the buttonholes.

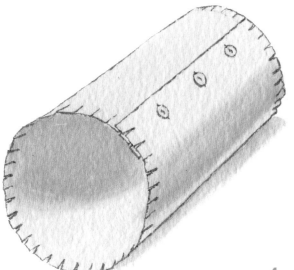

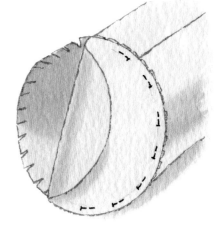

3 Snip the buttonholes open. Overlapping the fabric by 2-in, mark the button positions with pins and sew the three buttons in place on the underlap. Button the fabric to make an open-ended tube (you could also pin the fabric to hold it in place). Snip around each end at ½-in intervals, making each cut no more than ⅜-in deep. Turn wrong side out.

4 Cut two circles of fabric for the ends, adding a ½-in seam allowance all around. Right sides facing (you need to turn the tube inside out), pin the ends to the buttoned tube, and stitch together. Unbutton the cover and turn it right side out. Place the bolster pillow form inside the cover, and button the cover.

ribbon-tied pillow

Using a grommet kit, available from fabric or craft stores, provides a
quick and simple way to add decoration to a plain pillow cover.
Here, a navy blue cotton pillow cover has been embellished with a
pretty ribbon that crisscrosses its way down the pillow and is tied in
a neat bow at the base. It's also easy to change the ribbon if you
alter the decoration of your room.

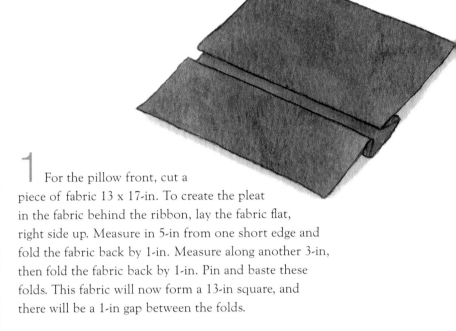

YOU WILL NEED

Fabric for pillow cover

Scissors

Pins

Sewing machine and thread

Grommet kit

Ribbon

12-in pillow form

1 For the pillow front, cut a piece of fabric 13 x 17-in. To create the pleat in the fabric behind the ribbon, lay the fabric flat, right side up. Measure in 5-in from one short edge and fold the fabric back by 1-in. Measure along another 3-in, then fold the fabric back by 1-in. Pin and baste these folds. This fabric will now form a 13-in square, and there will be a 1-in gap between the folds.

TIP

Instead of making the pillow cover, you could punch grommet holes in a store-bought cover and thread the ribbon through.

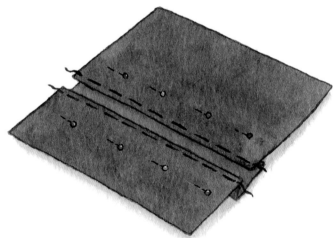

2 Mark the positions of the grommets with pins. Each grommet should be 1½-in away from the edge of the fold. Make the first pair 2-in down from the top edge of the fabric, then leave a 3-in gap between subsequent pairs. Following the instructions on the kit, insert the grommets.

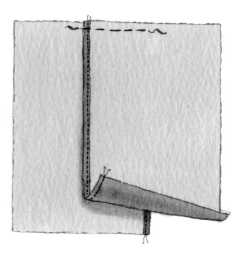

3 The back of the pillow has an envelope opening. Cut two rectangles of fabric, each 13 x 9-in. Fold, pin, and stitch a ½-in hem on one long edge of each rectangle. Overlap the two rectangles by 4-in, with the hemmed edges facing inward.

4 Pin and baste the overlapping pieces together just inside the top and bottom seamlines. This will make a 13-in square.

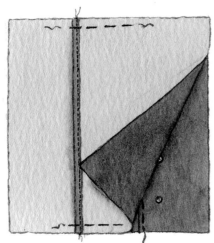

5 Place the front and back together, right sides facing. Pin all around, and stitch a ½-in seam. Trim the seam and corners. Remove the basting from the back and turn right side out.

6 Lace the ribbon through the grommets (lacing horizontally on the underside and diagonally on top); tie in a bow. Trim the ends, then stitch a narrow hem at each end. Insert the pillow form. Remove the basting holding the pleat in place.

organdy pillow

This delicate organdy pillow would look extremely elegant displayed on a bedroom chair or sitting atop a pile of crisp linen-covered pillows. It would make a perfect gift as you can choose the monogram to suit the recipient. Instead of using pearly seed beads, you could embroider a name or short message on the front.

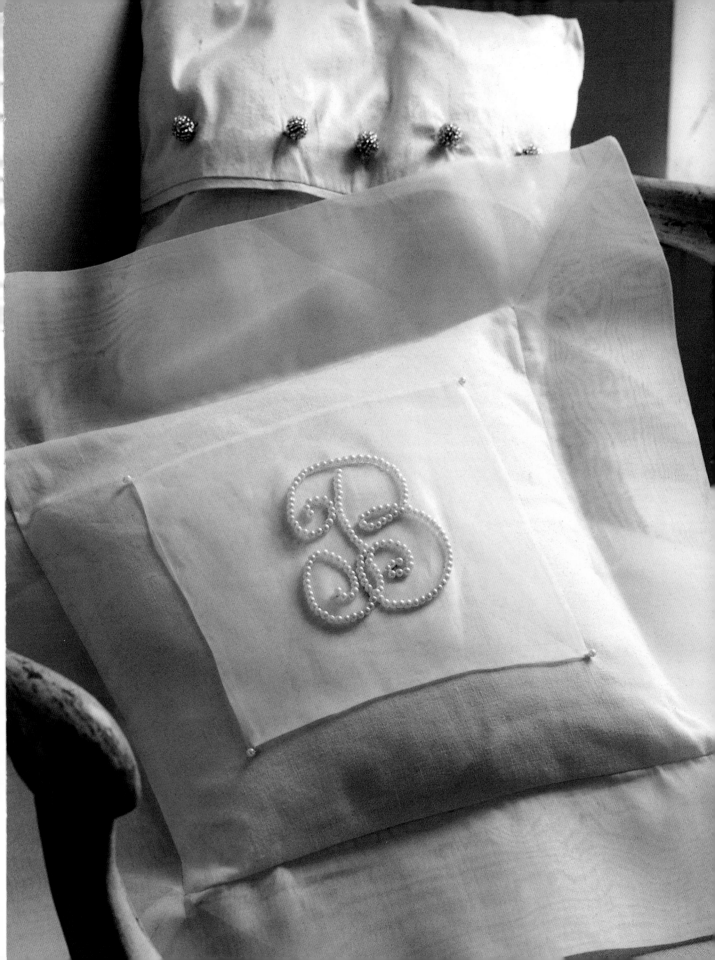

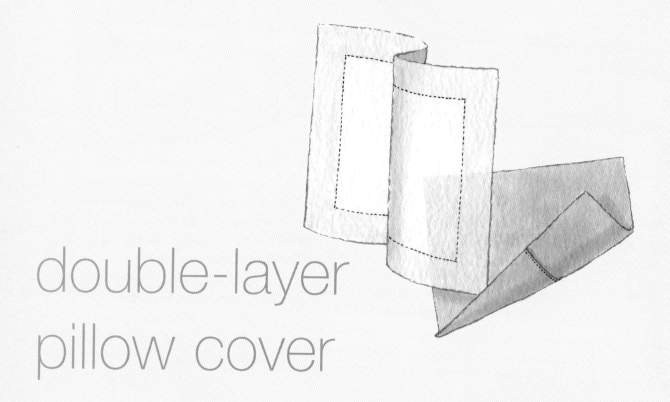

double-layer
pillow cover

The combination of an under layer of pale pink cotton and a gauzy, floating organdy top layer makes this pillow cover look extremely feminine and sophisticated. The crisp edging emphasizes the contrast between the two fabrics. A row of these pillows in a variety of sugared almond colors—the palest of greens, yellows, pinks, and blues—would look perfect lined up on a white sofa.

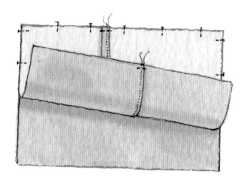

YOU WILL NEED

Pale pink cotton fabric

Tape measure

Scissors

Pins

Sewing machine and thread

Organdy

**Rectangular pillow form,
12 x 18-in**

1 To make the pink cover, cut a piece of fabric for the front 13 x 19-in. For the back, cut two pieces, each 13 x 12-in. Fold over, pin, and stitch a ½-in hem on one of the long edges of each back piece. Lay the front piece right side up. Place the two back pieces on top, right side down and with the hemmed edges overlapping so that the raw edges align with those of the front. Pin around all four sides. Stitch a ½-in seam all around. Trim the seam and corners, and turn the cover right side out.

TIP

A simple "envelope style" back avoids the need to fit zippers to such delicate fabric.

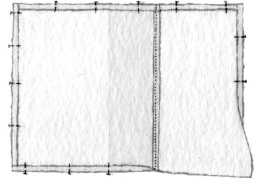

2 For the organdy back, cut two pieces 14 x 12-in. Fold, pin, press, and stitch a ½-in hem on one of the long edges of each back piece. Overlap the two hemmed edges to form a rectangle 14 x 20-in and pin the overlapping pieces together. Fold, pin, and press a ½-in hem all around.

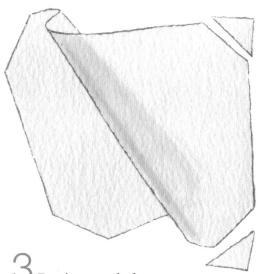

3 For the organdy front, cut
a piece 22 x 28-in. At each corner, measure in 5-in
along each edge and then fold in these corner
triangles toward the center. Cut ¼-in outside each
fold line to remove the corner triangles leaving ¼-in
seam allowances.

4 With ¼-in still folded in on each corner, find the
halfway point and mark it with a pin. Fold the
organdy between the pins to form the double layer of
edging, with diagonal folds at the corners. Press.

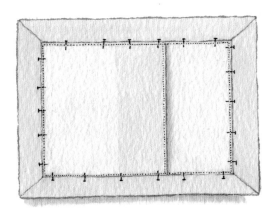

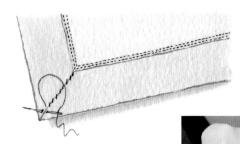

5 With the mitered side of the
organdy front facing upward, center
the organdy back over it, right side
up. The back will cover the raw edges
of the front. Pin all around, and
stitch close to the edge of the back.

6 Slipstitch the diagonal
folds on the mitered corners
together (by taking the
needle through the folds
alternately, with tiny stitches
in between). Place the pillow
form inside the pink cover,
then slip that inside the
organdy cover, with the
openings at the back.

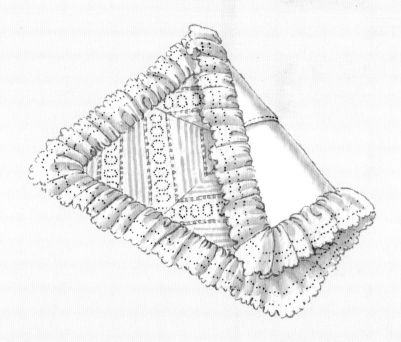

white lace pillow

This old-fashioned pillow cover is made from a piece of antique embroidered cotton, edged with a soft ruffle of matching cotton lace edging. This design is a good way to breathe new life into a damaged piece of fabric, as the pillow cover is pieced together like an easy form of patchwork. Here it is made with four large squares cut diagonally on the fabric, with a smaller central square.

YOU WILL NEED

Embroidered cotton fabric

Tape measure

Scissors

Pins

**Sewing machine,
or needle and thread**

White backing fabric

Cotton lace edging

12-in pillow form

TIP

If you only have smaller pieces of
fabric to work with, you could
create a similar effect by piecing
strips together in the style of log
cabin patchwork.

1 Cut four squares of
embroidered fabric, each
7 x 7-in. If you are using a
fabric with a horizontal
pattern, such as here, you
need to make sure all
pieces feature the same portion of the
pattern—it may be easiest to cut four pieces of
paper to the correct size and place them on the
fabric first, to ensure the patterns run in the
right direction.

2 Pin two squares together,
right sides facing, taking a ½-in
seam allowance and making sure the horizontal
patterns run at right angles to each other. Pin the
other two squares in the same way, then open out
the pinned pieces to double-check they will marry
up correctly.

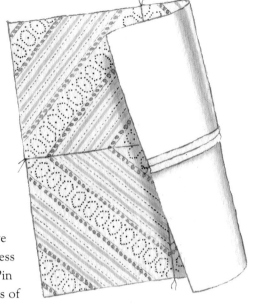

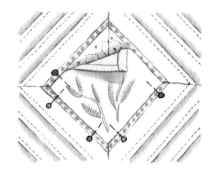

3 Sew along
the two pinned
seams, so you have
two rectangles. Press
the seams open. Pin
the two long edges of
the rectangles together,
open them up to check that the patterns run in the
right direction, then sew together to form the pillow
front. Press the seam open.

4 Cut a square of embroidered fabric
2 x 2-in. As this forms the center of the
pillow, you may be able to use an
embroidered motif if one appears on your
fabric. Fold and press a ¼-in hem on all sides.
Place the square diagonally over the center
of the pillow, pin, and stitch in place.

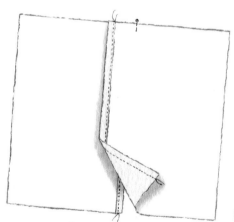

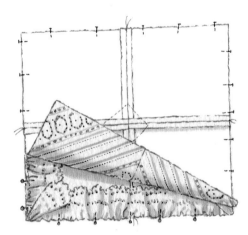

5 For the
back of the pillow, cut two pieces
of backing fabric 9 x 13-in. Fold over a ½-in hem
on one longer side of each rectangle; pin, press,
and stitch. Overlap the two rectangles by 4-in, with
the hemmed edges toward the center. This should
make a square the same size as the pillow front. Pin
together through the overlap.

6 On the right side of the pillow back, pin the lace
around the edge, with the ruffle pointing inward. Allow
extra fullness at the corners. At one corner, stitch the
two ends together and press the seam open. Place the
pillow front on top, right side down. Pin, sandwiching
the ruffle in between. Stitch a ½-in seam around all four
sides. Remove all the pins, turn right side out, press and
insert the pillow form through the opening in the back.

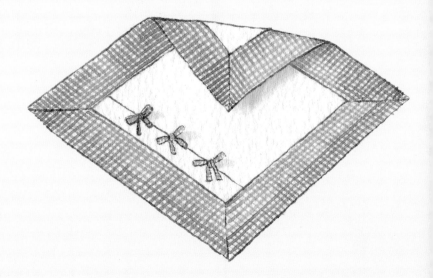

contrast-bordered pillow

Crisp white cotton partnered with a small-scale blue-and-white checked fabric is always a winning combination. A row of three neat ties, made from the contrasting border fabric, is used to secure the opening. The instructions given here are for a square pillow cover, but the design would work equally well as a pillow sham.

paneled pillow

This is an excellent way of making a little go a long way. A small remnant of fabric, left over from making curtains for this living room, has been used as a central panel on a pillow cover. This technique works best with fabrics with a strong motif or pattern and is a good way of linking soft furnishings.

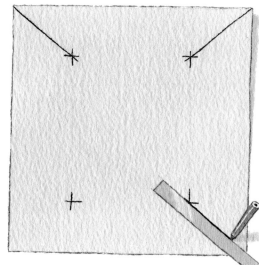

YOU WILL NEED

Fabric remnant with a strong motif

Fabric for the surround

Scissors

Pattern paper

Ruler

Fabric for the border and back

Bias binding to match the pillow cover fabric (see step 5)

Piping cord

Zipper

Sewing machine and thread

Pins

Pillow form

TIP

If you wish, you could stitch this panel, with or without the border, to a store-bought pillow cover.

1 Cut out the central motif for your pillow (here, a rectangle has been cut). Next, cut a piece of fabric for the surround—this should be at least 2-in wider and deeper than the motif. Cut a paper pattern for the central hole in the surround fabric—here it was easiest to draw a rectangle then soften the corners with curves. Place this pattern on the surround fabric and cut out the hole. Turn the raw edges under by ½-in, snipping into the seam allowance on the curved portions, and pin in place on top of the motif fabric. Slipstitch in place (see page 25, step 6).

2 To complete the pillow front, make a pattern for the four pieces of border. First, cut out a piece of paper the size of your pillow. Place the front panel on top of this, positioned centrally, and mark the corners of the panel on the paper. Draw diagonal lines from these four marks to the outer corners of the pillow. Label the areas for the two sides, the top, and the bottom pieces, then cut out the pattern pieces.

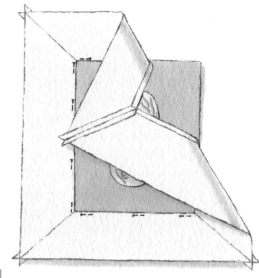

3 Cut out one piece of fabric for each pattern piece, adding ½-in all around for seam allowances. Pin two adjoining pieces together along the diagonal lines, right sides facing. Stitch, stopping ½-in from the inner edge. Add the third and fourth pieces in the same way. From the same fabric, cut a piece for the back, adding a ½-in seam allowance all around.

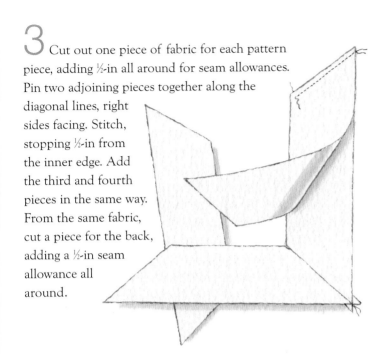

4 Fold under a ½-in seam on the inner edges, pin, and press. Position over the central panel and pin in place. Stitch around all four sides close to the edge. Press the seams flat.

5 To make the bias binding for the piping, cut a strip of fabric on the bias (diagonal), long enough to go around the pillow, plus 1-in, and wide enough to wrap around the cord, plus 1-in. If you need to join lengths of fabric, join them on the diagonal, as shown. For the piping, wrap the fabric around the cord, right side out, then machine stitch as close to the cord as possible, using the piping foot.

6 Place the pillow front right side up. Pin and then baste the piping all around, with the seam allowance pointing outward; clip

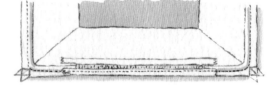

into the seam allowance at the corners. Place the zipper at the bottom, face down, with the teeth just covering the edge of the piping. Pin. Using the zipper foot, stitch the bottom tape in place, close to the teeth.

7 Turn over the zipper, turning under the seam allowance. Turn under and press the seam allowance at the bottom of the back

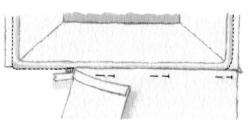

piece. With the back right side up, and the folded edge butting up to the folded edge of the front, pin the back to the other zipper tape. Topstitch alongside the teeth and across the ends of the zipper as far as the fold. Open the zipper. Place the front and back with right sides facing. Pin and stitch a ½-in seam on the remaining edges. Trim Corners. Turn right side out, press, and insert the pillow form.

bejeweled tieback

Curtain tiebacks offer such a simple solution to changing your window dressing. While it can be expensive and time-consuming to make new drapes, simply changing the tiebacks allows you to coordinate different colors or fabrics within a room, linking various elements within the décor. This striking tieback creates a decorative focal point in its own right.

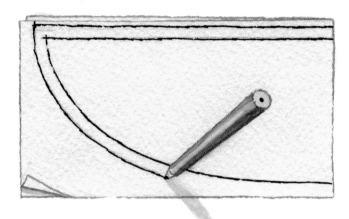

TIP

Before cutting the fabric, pin the paper pattern in place around the curtain to check that the tieback is long enough to hold the curtain in place without gathering up the fabric too tightly.

1 For a crescent-shaped tieback, fold the pattern paper in half and draw a half-crescent from the fold line outward, adding a ½-in seam allowance all around; cut out the pattern and unfold so you have a symmetrical shape. For a rectangular tieback, cut out a rectangle of the appropriate size from the pattern paper, allowing for a ½-in seam allowance all around. Place the pattern on the curtain fabric and cut out two pieces. Cut one piece of interfacing, without the seam allowance.

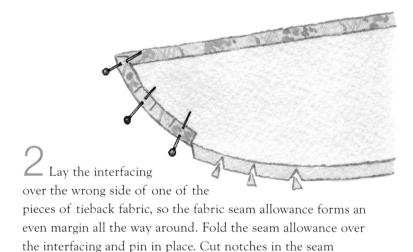

2 Lay the interfacing over the wrong side of one of the pieces of tieback fabric, so the fabric seam allowance forms an even margin all the way around. Fold the seam allowance over the interfacing and pin in place. Cut notches in the seam allowance to allow the fabric to lie flat against the interfacing. Press. Baste together and remove the pins.

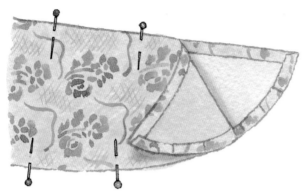

3 Fold in the seam allowance on the second piece of fabric, cutting notches as in step 2. Press, then place on top of the interfacing, right side up, and pin in place. Slipstitch around the edges (see page 25, step 6), and remove the basting stitches.

4 Sew the ornaments in place around the upper and lower edges. Sew a curtain ring to each end of the tieback, and fit a hook to the wall.

linen curtain

Cream linen drapes always look
supremely stylish, and their simplicity
means you can partner them with
almost any style of home furnishings.
This curtain could either be made from a
length of specially purchased linen, or as a way to reuse an old
linen sheet if you are lucky enough to have one. Ideal for summer
months, linen window treatments allow light into the room, yet
cut out the glare of the sun. Simple ribbon ties and an integral
valance provide a fresh and pretty top treatment.

window screen

A screen placed in front of a window is an elegantly tailored
alternative to a curtain or shade. The trick is to choose a fine
fabric that will allow light through, yet still provide privacy.
Here a fine voile patterned with colorful butterflies has been
used—when bright sunshine pours through the window, the
butterflies will appear to be hovering in the air. Organdy (either
plain or with an embroidered pattern) would also work well,
and in winter you could replace the sheer fabric with panels of
velvet to create instant warmth.

YOU WILL NEED

Screen frame

Sheer fabric

Tape measure

Scissors

Sewing machine and thread

Pins

Ribbon

TIP

This frame has pairs of metal bars through which the fabric panels can slide. Alternatively, you could sew additional ties to the sides and base of the fabric to hold it to the frame, or use a staple gun to attach the fabric to a wooden frame.

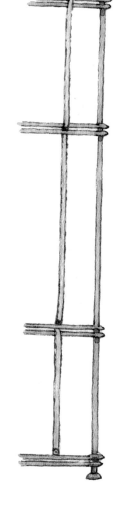

1 Measure the width and height of each panel. For each, cut out a piece of fabric measuring twice the width, plus 1½-in, by the height, plus 1½-in.

2 Fold the fabric in half lengthwise, right sides facing. Pin together, and stitch a ¾-in seam around the top and side. Trim the corners.

3 Turn right side out, and
press. Turn under and press
¼-in along the bottom edges;
slipstitch the bottom closed
(see page 25, step 6).

4 Cut two 12-in lengths of ribbon. Fold in
half and stitch each to one of the top corners,
through the center fold on the ribbon. Feed the
fabric through the bars on the frame and tie the
top corners to the frame. Trim the ribbon ends
on the diagonal to prevent raveling.

chapter two

chair covers

striped cushion pads

Pink candy-stripes on a fresh white background bring a modern, informal touch to this serene dining room decorated in cool shades of gray and white. Armed with a staple gun, you can easily give dining chairs with drop-in seats an instant facelift with new fabric covers. When using a strong pattern such as this, the most important thing is to cut and position the fabric so that the stripes are central and all seats display the same area of pattern. Unless the existing seats are very worn or the fabric is very thick, you can usually lay the new fabric over the old.

YOU WILL NEED

**Scrap fabric, to make
a template**

Pins

Scissors

Fabric

Staple gun

1 To remove the seat
pad, turn the dining chair
upside down and look at the
fixings. On some chairs you can
simply tap hard on the base of the
seat and the pad will pop out; on
other chairs you may need to use a
screwdriver to release holding screws.
Using the scrap fabric, make a template. Pin the scrap fabric tightly
over the seat pad and cut out, adding a 3-in allowance all around.

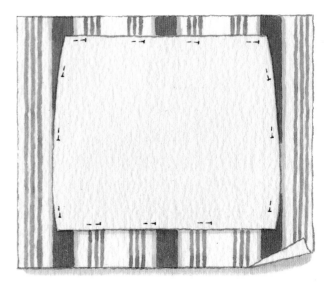

TIP

Make sure the fabric you choose
for seat covers is reasonably
hardwearing and can be sponged
down if spillages occur.

2 Place the template on the fabric and decide where you want the
pattern to appear. Cut out the fabric.

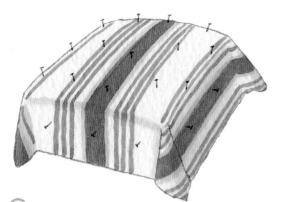

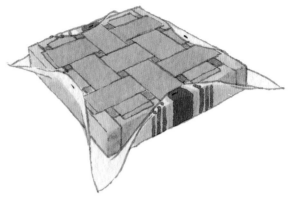

3 Place the fabric over the seat pad, pulling the fabric taut, and stab a few pins through to the pad to hold the fabric in position.

4 Turn the pad over and staple the fabric just once in the center of each of the four sides. Turn the pad back again and double-check the pattern is still properly centered and the fabric is pulled tight.

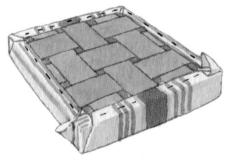

5 Turn the pad face down again and continue stapling. It is best to add a few staples either side of the first four applied in the previous step, and then work into the four corners. Constantly check that the pattern is central and that the fabric is taut. To miter each corner, pull the fabric diagonally over the corner; staple, then fold the excess at each side into a pleat, and staple.

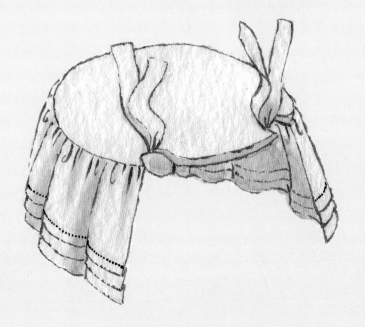

organdy chair skirt

A gauzy skirt of finest organdy, studded with glistening pearls, turns an everyday dining chair into the prettiest of seats, perfect for the boudoir or dressing room. A thin foam pad, encased in plain white cotton, softens the hard wooden seat, while tucks along the lower edge add body to the skirt.

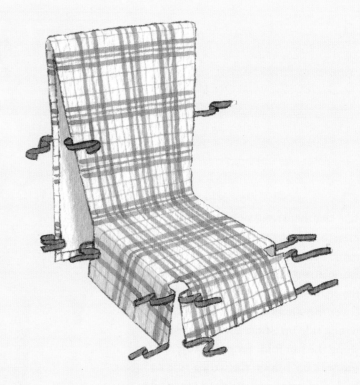

simple slipcovers

These contemporary blue-and-white plaid slipcovers

dress up chairs in an instant, and provide the perfect way to

coordinate mismatching furniture. The covers are far easier and

quicker to make than traditional upholstery—just one length of

fabric folds over the back of the chair and continues over the

seat. It is held in place with ties at the side. If you are using a

fabric with a dominant pattern (such as this bold plaid or a

large floral pattern), take time to position the fabric carefully so

that the pattern is centered on the chair back and seat.

YOU WILL NEED

Tape measure

Fabric

Pattern paper

Scissors

Sewing machine and thread

Pins

Solid-color fabric, for the ties

TIP

Make sure the fabric you choose for the ties is not too thick, because after folding and stitching it still needs to be flexible enough to be tied into bows. Alternatively, use lengths of strong ribbon, which can simply be sewn in place after the ends are hemmed to prevent raveling.

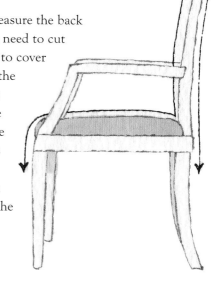

1 Using a tape measure, measure the back and the seat of the chair. You need to cut a piece of fabric long enough to cover both sides of the chair back, the seat, and the front of the seat cushion. The fabric should be wide enough to drape over the sides of the seat cushion. It is safest to cut a paper pattern first. As with the chair shown here, you may need to shape the pattern around the chair legs

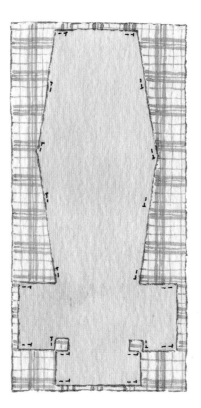

2 Cut out the paper pattern, adding an extra ½-in all around for hemming. Lay the pattern on the fabric, positioning it so that any dominant pattern is centered on the chair back and seat. Cut out the fabric.

62

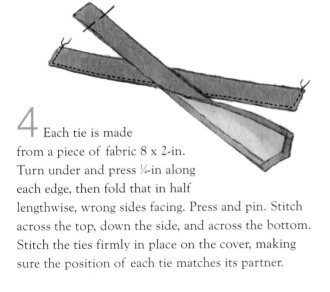

3 Lay the fabric over the chair to ensure that it fits. Zigzag stitch the raw edges. Turn under, pin, press, and stitch a ½-in hem all around, clipping into the inner corners within the seam allowance. Place the slipcover on the chair and mark the position of the side ties with pins.

4 Each tie is made from a piece of fabric 8 x 2-in. Turn under and press ¼-in along each edge, then fold that in half lengthwise, wrong sides facing. Press and pin. Stitch across the top, down the side, and across the bottom. Stitch the ties firmly in place on the cover, making sure the position of each tie matches its partner.

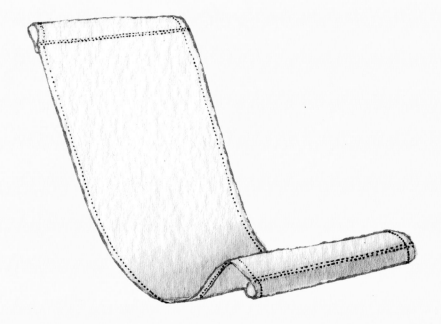

deckchair slings

This is such a quick and easy way to give your deckchairs a facelift for summer. The traditional, sturdy wooden frames often outlast the canvas slings, but it's really very simple to stitch a new sling. You may even wish to revarnish the wooden frame or repaint it in a color to complement the canvas.

Tape measure

Strong, preshrunk canvas

Scissors

Pins

Sewing machine, or sturdy
needle and strong thread

Staple gun (optional)

1 Unscrew the top and
bottom horizontal wooden bars
holding the existing canvas in place.
Measure the width and length of the existing
canvas sling. Add hem allowances of 1-in to each
side and 4-in to the top and to the bottom. Cut
out the canvas to this size. Turn under, pin, press,
and stitch a 1-in hem down each side. Then turn
under, pin, press, and stitch a ½-in hem at the top
and bottom.

TIP

If the deckchair cannot be
dismantled, cut away the old canvas
and use a staple gun to attach the
new sling to the wooden bars.
Some fabric stores sell canvas
woven in special widths especially
for deckchairs, which means there's
no need to hem the sides.

2 To make each channel for the two wooden
bars, measure around the bar and add ½-in to this
measurement. Turn under the fabric, pin, and stitch
the channel in place. Stitch another two or three
lines across the width of the canvas to
make the sling strong enough to
hold an adult.

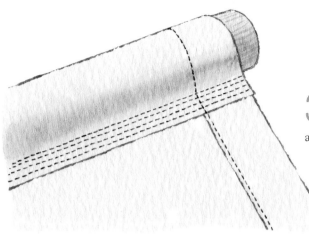

3 Slide the wooden bars through the channels and reattach to the deckchair frame.

4 A new canvas sling for a footstool can be made in exactly the same way, either by sewing channels for the wooden support bars or by using a staple gun to attach the canvas to the frame.

Chut ... bébé dort ...

Hush ... baby sleeps ...

mes souliers

bed linen and accessories

fitted headboard cover

This headboard cover simply slips over the existing padded headboard like a snugly fitting sleeve. It's the ideal way to give the bed a whole new look, and you could make two different covers to match both winter and summer drapes. Any leftover fabric could be made into covers for throw pillows for the room.

YOU WILL NEED

Tape measure

Piping cord

Fabric for piping casing

Scissors

Sewing machine with piping foot and thread

Pattern paper

Fabric for cover

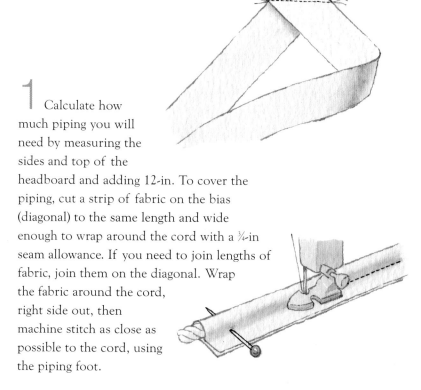

1 Calculate how much piping you will need by measuring the sides and top of the headboard and adding 12-in. To cover the piping, cut a strip of fabric on the bias (diagonal) to the same length and wide enough to wrap around the cord with a ¾-in seam allowance. If you need to join lengths of fabric, join them on the diagonal. Wrap the fabric around the cord, right side out, then machine stitch as close as possible to the cord, using the piping foot.

TIP

If using an expensive fabric for covering the headboard, you could use a plain fabric such as calico for the back if it won't be seen. It's best if this is of a similar weight to the main fabric and you may wish to launder it before cutting out, just in case it shrinks.

2 Measure the height and depth of the headboard, and add ½-in seam allowances all around. If the headboard has a slightly curved top, as in this photo, it is probably best to make a paper pattern before cutting the fabric. If the headboard reaches to the floor, you may need to take any fittings into consideration. As this cover does not include a side gusset, add twice the thickness of any padding on the headboard to the width measurement.

3 Cut out the front and back pieces for the cover. If using a fabric with a dominant pattern, position the pattern carefully on the fabric to avoid cutting through motifs at the top of the headboard.

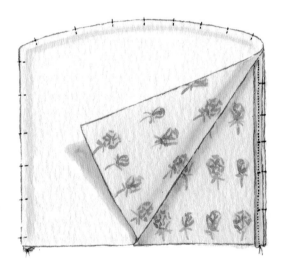

4 Lay the front piece right side up. Pin piping all around the sides and top, with the corded edge facing inward and the fabric raw edges facing out. Clip into the piping seam allowance at the corners. Baste in place. Lay the back piece on top, right side down, enclosing the piping, and pin in place. Stitch all around the three sides. Fold, pin, press, and stitch a hem around the lower edges, then slip the cover onto the headboard.

tied
headboard cover

This is such a quick and easy way to soften the appearance of a metal or wooden bedstead. A length of fabric, chosen to complement the bed linen, is hemmed and draped over the horizontal bar of the headboard. Decorative ribbons at the sides hold the fabric in place and add a pretty finishing touch at the same time. You could easily make a number of these headboard covers, to match each set of bed linen, or use the same fabric for the curtains.

YOU WILL NEED

Tape measure

Fabric

Scissors

Pins

**Sewing machine,
or needle and thread**

Ribbon

1 Measure the width of the bed frame (you need the length of the horizontal rail) and add a hem allowance of 2-in to this measurement. For the length of fabric required, measure the distance from the deck, up over the top horizontal rail, and then down to the floor or just below the mattress (depending on the desired height of the lower edge) and add 2-in to this measurement.

TIP

If you like to prop yourself up in bed to read, make this headboard cover more comfortable by adding a thick layer of batting underneath the fabric, or fold a spare blanket over the headboard before tying the cover in place.

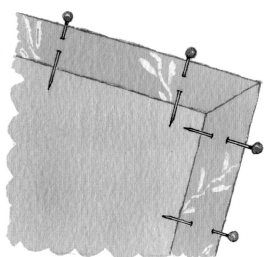

2 Cut out the fabric to this size. Turn under a double ½-in hem on all four sides, pin, and press. Stitch.

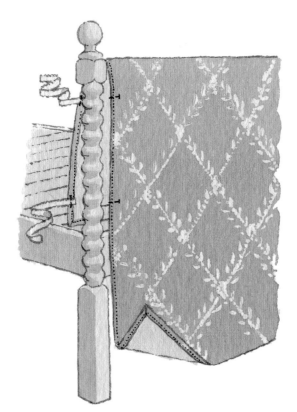

3 Place the hemmed fabric in position over the headboard. Decide the positions of the ribbon ties and mark the places with pins.

4 Cut the ribbon ties. You can either cut lengths which are just long enough to tie into bows (about 8-in) or cut much longer ribbons for more decorative bows which can drape down to the floor. Pin and then stitch the ribbons in place. Tie into bows, then trim the ends diagonally to prevent fraying.

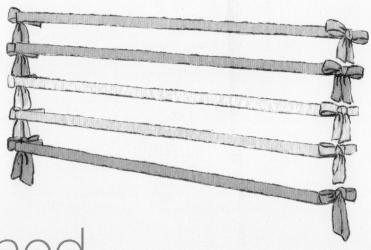

beribboned headboard

This is such a simple way to jazz up a plain padded headboard.

Bands of good-quality ribbon, in colors chosen to match the

bed linen, are stitched across the width of the headboard, while

separate bows are sewn to the sides. If you wish to make the

headboard cover, follow the directions for the fitted headboard

cover on page 70, then simply decorate the front with ribbons

before attaching the back piece.

YOU WILL NEED

Tape measure

Lengths of ribbon, in your
choice of colors

Tailor's chalk (optional)

Pins

Scissors

Needle and thread, to match
the ribbon colors

1 Decide where you want
the ribbon bands to be
stitched and carefully measure
down from the top of the
headboard, marking where the
top edge of the ribbon should
be stitched, with either pins
or tailor's chalk. It is important
to measure accurately so the ribbons are stitched
horizontally and not at a slight angle. Take into account
the height of the pillows.

TIP

For a quick and easy version of this
project, use strips of fusible web to
permanently bond the ribbon to the
headboard cover, following the
manufacturer's instructions.

2 Cut the first ribbon
the width of the bedhead
plus the sides and a 1-in
hem. Turn under ½-in at
one end and pin the ribbon
across the headboard, turning under the hem at the other
side. It is probably easiest to "stab" the pins at an angle into
the padding of the headboard. Double-check that the ribbon
is perfectly horizontal. Slipstitch the top of the ribbon in
place (see page 36, step 1), then slipstitch the lower edge.
Repeat with the remaining bands of ribbon.

3 Cut a 24-in length of ribbon to make each bow. Fold a narrow hem at each end and slipstitch. (If you wish, you could cut the ribbon ends on the diagonal before hemming.)

4 Tie each ribbon in a large bow. Pin the bows in place on the sides of the headboard, and sew firmly in place.

gathered lampshade

A candlestick-style lamp base is given a new lease of life with a softly gathered linen cover which sits on top of the original shade. Here a striped linen has been used and the fabric cut so the white stripe appears as a band toward the bottom of the shade and on the top and bottom edges; if you use a solid-color fabric, you could easily stitch a band of decorative ribbon onto the fabric before gathering it up.

YOU WILL NEED

Lampshade and base

Tape measure

Scissors

Linen fabric

Pins

**Sewing machine,
or needle and thread**

Elastic, ¼-in wide

Safety pin

Short length of ribbon

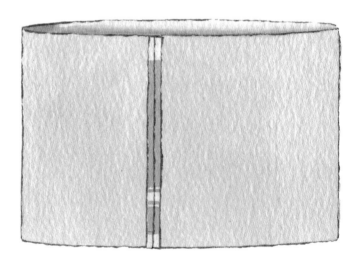

1 Measure the
circumference of the
lower, wider edge of the
lampshade. Measure
down the side of the
lampshade to find the depth. Add 8-in
to the circumference measurement,
and 4-in to the depth measurement.
Cut out a rectangle of fabric to this size. If using a
striped fabric, remember to position the stripe
before cutting out the rectangle.

2 Fold the fabric in half, short ends together
and right sides facing. Pin the short ends together,
with a seam allowance of ½-in. Stitch the seam,
then press it open. You now have a wide tube
of fabric with raw edges.

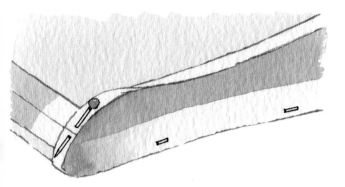

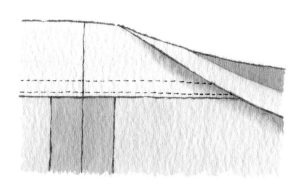

3 With the tube of fabric wrong side out, turn up, pin, press, and sew a double ¼-in hem along one edge. This will be the lower edge of the lampshade.

4 Fold over 2-in of the top edge, pin, and press. Stitch along the lower edge of this folded fabric, and then complete another row of stitching ½-in above this, to create a channel for the elastic.

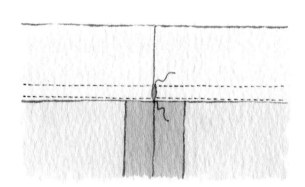

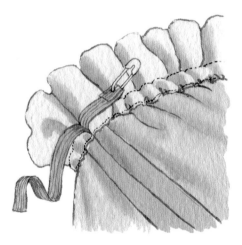

5 Carefully unpick a few stitches in the side seam by the channel. You need to make a gap just large enough to thread the elastic through.

6 Attach the safety pin to one end of the elastic and use it to feed the elastic all the way through the channel. Pull up the elastic until the cover fits over the shade. Cut off the excess elastic and sew the ends together. Push them inside and hand-sew the opening. Tie the ribbon in a bow and sew it to the gathers.

dressing table skirt

A full skirt of striped black-and-white fabric is the perfect way to bring this fifties-style, kidney-shaped dressing table right up to date. Simply changing the fabric can give a completely different look to a room—checked gingham would provide a country feel, these stripes give a cool, contemporary look, while a floral-patterned fabric would add a distinctly feminine touch.

YOU WILL NEED

Tape measure

Scissors

Fabric

Pins

Sewing machine and thread

Staple gun

Ribbon, at least ½-in wide

White craft glue

TIP

If you are using striped fabric for the skirt, make sure the stripes run in the correct direction before cutting the fabric.

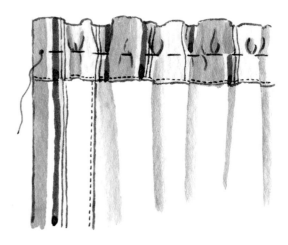

1 Measure around the top edge of the dressing table and double the measurement. Measure the height of the dressing table and add 2-in. Cut out a piece of fabric to this size. Fold under, pin, press, and stitch a 1-in hem on all four sides. Sew a row or two of gathering stitches along the top of the fabric, ½-in from the top, then gently gather up the fabric to fit around the dressing table.

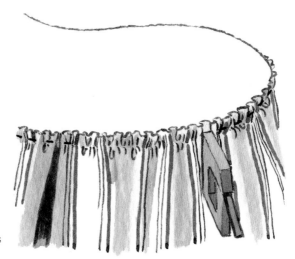

2 Drape the fabric around the dressing table (you could use low-tack tape to hold it in place temporarily). Using the staple gun, attach the two ends to the center back of the table. Adjust the gathers so they fall evenly, then staple the fabric all the way around.

3 Cut a length of ribbon to fit all around the table and carefully glue in place to hide the staples and the gathering stitches.

4 Finally, make a flat ribbon bow and either glue or staple it to the front of the dressing table.

drawstring
scented sachet

This pretty drawstring fabric sachet is perfect for filling with dried rose petals, lavender heads, or mixed potpourri. Hang it either from the headboard to scent the bedroom or inside the closet to add a gentle perfume to clothes. If filled with lavender, it will help keep moths at bay. Replace the potpourri or flower heads as soon as the scent begins to fade.

YOU WILL NEED

Scissors

Fabric remnants for the bag
and contrasting top edge

Lace edging

Sewing machine, or needle and
thread

Pins

Ribbon

Safety pin

Decorative button

1 Cut out two 4 x 6-in rectangles of fabric for the bag. If you are using a fabric with a dominant motif (as used here), position the motif centrally on each side of the bag. Trim the bottom corners at an angle of 45 degrees, to make the curved bottom.

TIP

These drawstring sachets could also be used as giftbags, to enclose small presents for friends.

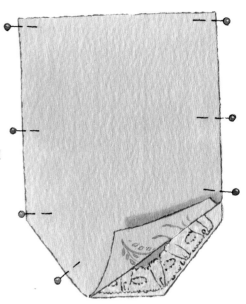

2 Pin the pieces of fabric together, right sides facing and with the lace sandwiched between them around the bottom curve as shown. Sew a ½-in seam around the sides and bottom. Press the seams open, turn right side out, and press.

3 Cut two 4 x 3-in rectangles of contrasting fabric for the top edging. Fold, pin, press, and stitch a ½-in hem down each short edge. Fold one fabric piece in half lengthwise, wrong sides facing, and pin it to one half of the bag at the top, enclosing ½-in of the raw edge of the bag. Topstitch in place. Repeat for the other fabric piece.

4 Cut two 4-in lengths of ribbon. Pin one on top of the seam joining the main bag and one contrasting fabric piece, turning under ½-in at each end of the ribbon. Carefully stitch along the top and bottom edges of the ribbon to create a channel for the ribbon drawstring. Leave both ends of the channel open. Attach the second ribbon to the other contrasting fabric piece in the same way.

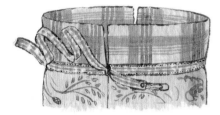

5 Cut a long length of ribbon for the handle. Attach the safety pin to one end and feed the ribbon through the entire channel, leaving a long loop on each side. Knot the two ends together securely.

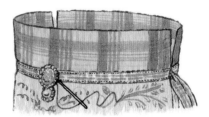

6 Sew a decorative button to the ribbon channel, making sure you only sew through the channel and not through the ribbon drawstring.

shoe sachets

Have you ever splurged more money than you can possibly justify on a pair of must-have dream shoes? To assuage your feelings of guilt, the least you can do is to look after them properly. These scented sachets have tapered ends so you can push them into the toes of your shoes to help them keep their shape, and are filled with lavender to keep them smelling sweet. When the lavender loses its aroma, simply refill the sachet with fresh herbs or potpourri.

YOU WILL NEED

Fabric

Scissors

Tailor's chalk

Ruler

Pins

**Sewing machine,
or needle and thread**

Scrap paper

Fabric paint

Fine paintbrush

Dried lavender

Ribbon

TIP

Use any leftover fabric to make a simple drawstring bag to store the shoes in, to prevent them from getting dusty or becoming scuffed in the closet.

1 For each sachet cut out two rectangles of fabric 8 x 4-in. To make the tapered toe, use tailor's chalk to make a mark halfway down one long side and another mark 1-in in from the corner on one short side. Join the two marks and cut along the line. Repeat on the other side, and use this as a pattern to taper the remaining rectangles.

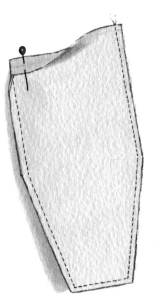

2 Place the two pieces of fabric together, right sides facing. Pin and stitch a ½-in seam around the sides and toe. Turn over a ½-in hem along the top edge and stitch, using a long, wide zigzag stitch and thread in a contrasting color. Turn right side out.

3 Place a piece of scrap paper inside the sachet to prevent the paint from leaking through. Paint your chosen design onto the fabric and leave to dry. (Some fabric paints need to be pressed with a warm iron to fix them—follow the instructions supplied with the paint.) Remove the scrap paper. Alternatively, you could embroider the design.

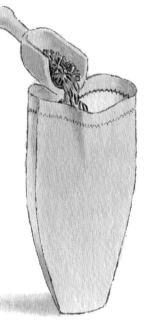

4 Half-fill the bag with dried lavender, and then tie a length of pretty ribbon tightly around the top to secure.

initialed linen sachets

These charming herb-filled linen sachets would make a perfect gift, and you can personalize them using the recipient's monogram. They are ideal for tucking into closets, drawers, and linen chests, to ward off moths and keep fabrics gently fragranced. The monograms are stamped onto heavyweight linen using a store-bought stamp, but if you wish, you could either paint them freehand or embroider the monogram or name. Small, brightly colored beads are sewn onto each corner as a decorative touch.

YOU WILL NEED

Heavyweight linen

Ruler

Scissors

Initial stamp

Fabric paint

Fine paintbrush

Scrap paper

Small beads

Pins

Sewing machine,
or needle and thread

Batting

Dried scented herbs

TIP

Instead of beads at the corners, you
could add an edging of eyelet lace.
Simply sandwich it between the two
layers in step 3, with the lace edge
facing inward.

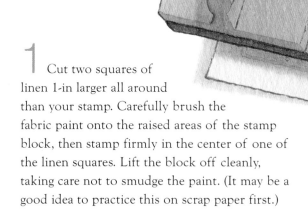

1 Cut two squares of
linen 1-in larger all around
than your stamp. Carefully brush the
fabric paint onto the raised areas of the stamp
block, then stamp firmly in the center of one of
the linen squares. Lift the block off cleanly,
taking care not to smudge the paint. (It may be a
good idea to practice this on scrap paper first.)

2 Leave the paint to dry.
Some fabric paints need to
be pressed on the wrong side
with a warm iron to set the
paint—check the instructions
on the paint pot.

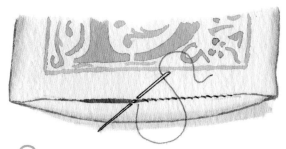

3 When the paint is dry, place the two linen squares together, right sides facing. Pin and stitch a ½-in hem around the top and two sides. Trim the corners. Turn right side out. Stuff the sachet with batting and dried herbs. Turn under and press ½-in on the raw edges, and slipstitch (see page 25, step 6).

4 Sew a colored bead onto each of the corners. If you wish, you could attach a length of ribbon to each top corner so the sachet can be hung around the neck of a coathanger.

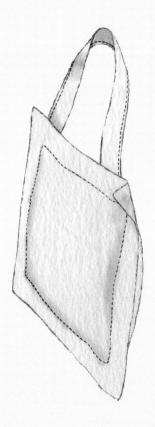

baby's pillow

This pretty mint-green pillow provides a stylish way to warn visitors and family to tread quietly past the nursery. It would make a lovely gift for sleep-deprived new parents wishing to take a nap and make the most of those precious moments when all is quiet and their baby slumbers. During waking hours the pillow can be hung from the end of a newborn baby's cradle or crib.

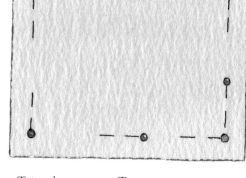

YOU WILL NEED

Ruler or yardstick

Scissors

Fabric

Pins

Sewing machine and thread

Scrap paper

Fabric paint

Fine paintbrush

Batting

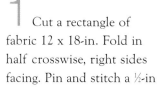 Cut a rectangle of fabric 12 x 18-in. Fold in half crosswise, right sides facing. Pin and stitch a ½-in seam down the two short sides. Trim the corners. Turn right side out and press. The folded edge will be the bottom of the pillow. With a row of pins, mark an inner stitching line 1-in from the bottom and sides, and starting and stopping 1½-in from the open top. Baste along this line, leaving the top open.

TIP

If you wish, rather than painting a message on the fabric, you could embroider it. Trace the words first with tailor's chalk.

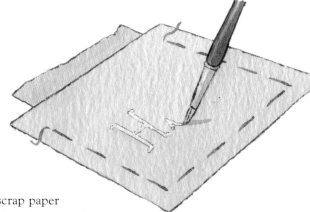

2 Slip a piece of scrap paper inside the pillow, so that the paint does not leak through to the back fabric. Paint your chosen wording within the rectangle marked by the basting. Allow the paint to dry thoroughly. (Some fabric paints need to be pressed with a warm iron to fix them—check the instructions on the paint pot.) Remove the scrap paper.

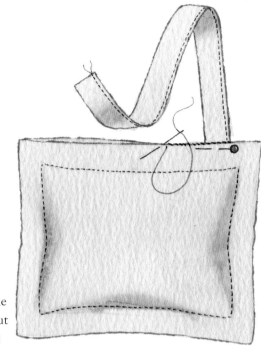

3 Starting at a point 1½-in from the top edge and one-third of the way along the top, stitch parallel to the top edge, then follow the basting down one side, along the bottom, and up the other side. Continue 1½-in from the top, stopping one-third of the way along the top, so that there is a gap in the center of the top edge. Remove the basting. Stuff the pillow with batting, then neatly stitch the gap closed.

4 To make the hanging strap, cut a piece of fabric 3 x 20-in. Fold the two long edges in toward the center, then fold in half again, so the raw edges are enclosed. Pin together, press, then topstitch. Turn in ½-in on the raw top edges of the back, pin, and press. Slip the two ends of the strap between the front and back edges; pin in place. Slipstitch the top edge closed (see page 25, step 6).

fabric-covered picture frames

Mismatching picture frames can be given a soft new look by covering them all in a solid-color fabric, with a matching ribbon used instead of picture wire. This is a good way to embellish inexpensive wooden frames. Solid-color fabrics work best as they will not detract from the picture. Choose colors to blend with the artwork you are framing.

YOU WILL NEED

Plain wooden frame

Paper and pen

Ruler

Scissors

Fabric

White craft glue

Ribbon

Staple gun

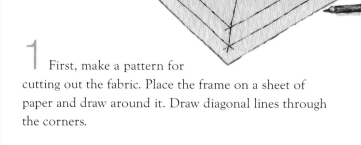

1 First, make a pattern for cutting out the fabric. Place the frame on a sheet of paper and draw around it. Draw diagonal lines through the corners.

TIP

Choose a heavy, close-weave fabric for this project. This will cover any imperfections in the frame and the glue will not seep through.

2 Cut along the diagonal lines to form four pattern pieces. Lay the pattern pieces on the fabric and cut out, adding a ½-in seam allowance all around.

3 Smear a thin layer of glue along the front of
one side of the frame. Fold under the seam
allowance on the diagonal edges of the
corresponding piece of fabric and place in position
on the frame. Wrap the fabric around the inner and
outer edges of the frame, and glue to the back. (You
will probably need to trim off some of the fabric to
prevent it from becoming too bulky.)

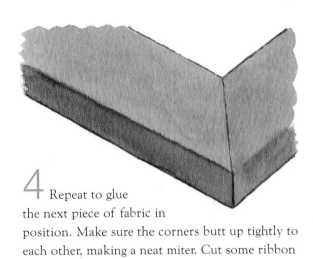

4 Repeat to glue
the next piece of fabric in
position. Make sure the corners butt up tightly to
each other, making a neat miter. Cut some ribbon
to the desired length and, using a staple gun,
attach it securely to the back of the frame toward
the top of the sides.

table linen and accessories

gathered tablecloth

A generous skirt of gathered pink silk brings a touch of luxury to this entrance hall. This is a neat trick for turning a plain or ugly table into something really special, as the fullness of the cloth hides any horrors lurking beneath the fabric. The cloth is made slightly longer than the table so it can flare out at the base. The top edge of the tablecloth is edged in matching piping for the perfect finishing touch.

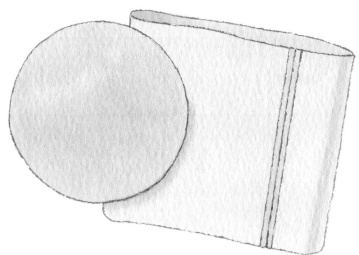

YOU WILL NEED

Tape measure

Scissors

Silk or taffeta

Pins

**Sewing machine,
with piping foot**

Needle and thread

Piping cord

1 Measure the tabletop and cut out a circle of fabric to this size plus a ½-in seam allowance all around. Measure and make a note of the tabletop's circumference. Measure and cut out the fabric for the skirt—this needs to be the height of the table plus 4-in, and 1½ times the circumference. Pin the two short edges of the skirt together, right sides facing and taking a ½-in seam allowance. Stitch the seam together and press open.

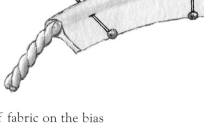

2 Cut a length of piping cord to the circumference measurement, plus 3-in. To cover the piping, cut a strip of fabric on the bias (diagonal) to the same length and wide enough to wrap around the cord with a ¾-in seam allowance. If you need to join lengths of fabric, join them on the diagonal. Wrap the fabric around the cord, right side out, then machine stitch as close as possible to the cord, using the piping foot.

114

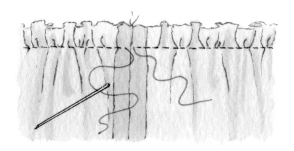

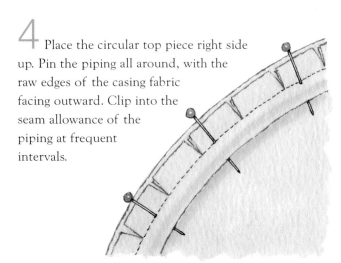

4 Place the circular top piece right side up. Pin the piping all around, with the raw edges of the casing fabric facing outward. Clip into the seam allowance of the piping at frequent intervals.

3 Thread the needle with a long piece of thread and sew one or two rows of gathering stitches around the top edge of the skirt, about ½-in from the edge. Gently pull the thread to gather the skirt until it matches the circumference of the table.

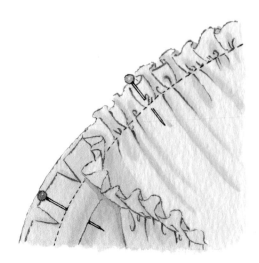

5 To join the piping, unpick the casing fabric on one side and cut away the cord so the two ends butt up. Fold the unpicked casing fabric over the join and trim to ¼-in. Fold under ½-in and pin. Baste the piping in place.

6 Place the skirt on top, wrong side up, with the raw gathered edge even with the edge of the top piece. Pin, taking a ½-in seam allowance. Adjust the gathers so they are even. Stitch. Trim the seam allowances to different widths to make the seam less bulky. Place the cloth on the table and pin a double hem (you can decide how much you want the skirt to flare out). Press and stitch.

organdy tablecloth

This elegant glass-topped side table boasts two contrasting cloths—an overlong underskirt of fine embroidered cotton topped with an elegant bordered organdy cloth, the sharp angles of the overcloth providing a strong contrast to the flowing lines of the underskirt. These two very different styles can be successfully combined because both cloths contain the same sophisticated shades of gold.

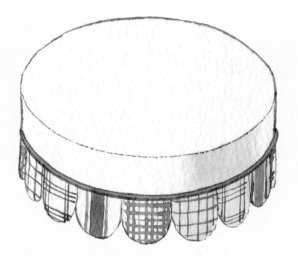

scallop-edged
tablecloth

Made in classic kitchen colors of blue and white, this fitted linen

tablecloth has a decorative scalloped edge trimmed with navy

blue piping. Here the scallops have been cut from blue-and-white

dish towels in a mixture of checks and stripes. As the cloth is

made to fit snugly around the table, it would be a good idea to

launder all the fabrics before cutting and stitching them together,

just in case of shrinkage.

1 Measure the tabletop and cut out a circle of linen to this size, plus a ½-in seam allowance all around. For the side piece, measure the circumference of the table and cut out a rectangle of linen to this length plus 1-in, and with a depth of 6-in.

YOU WILL NEED

Tape measure

Heavy cream linen

Navy blue bias binding (see step 2)

Scissors

Sewing machine, with piping foot

Thread

Piping cord

Pins

Pattern paper

Selection of blue-and-white dish towels

2 For the bias binding, cut a length of navy fabric on the bias (diagonal), as long as the circumference of the table, plus 1-in, and wide enough to wrap around the cord with a ½-in seam allowance. If you need to join lengths of fabric, join them on the diagonal. For the piping, wrap the bias binding around the cord, right side out. Machine stitch as close to the cord as possible, using the piping foot.

TIP

This scalloped tablecloth would look extremely stylish used with the simple plaid slipcovers featured on page 60.

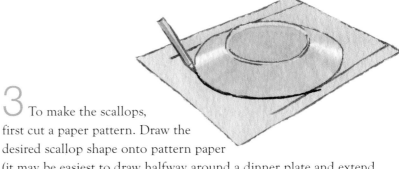

3 To make the scallops, first cut a paper pattern. Draw the desired scallop shape onto pattern paper (it may be easiest to draw halfway around a dinner plate and extend the sides). Allow a ½-in seam allowance all around. Make sure that the width of the scallop will allow you to edge the cloth with complete scallops without any gaps between them.

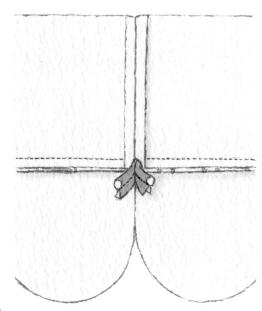

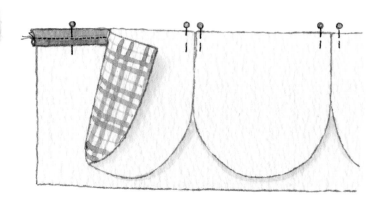

4 For each scallop, cut out two pieces of dish-towel fabric. Pin them together, right sides facing and taking a ½-in seam. Stitch around the sides and curved bottom of each scallop. Clip into the curves within the seam allowance, then turn right side out, and press.

5 Pin the piping to the right side of the linen rectangle, with the seam allowance facing outward. Pin the scallops in place, with the curved bottoms facing inward and making sure the different patterns are evenly spaced. Sew in place.

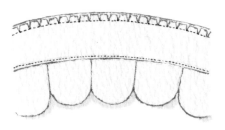

6 Pin the two ends of the scallop-edged rectangle together, right sides facing, taking a ½-in seam. Stitch together from the top down as far as the piping. When you reach the piping, unpick a few stitches on the fabric casing at each end, and trim the cord so both ends butt together neatly. Fold the fabric casing neatly to enclose the cord and hand-sew together. Press the seam flat.

7 Pin the scalloped side edging to the linen circle, right sides facing and raw edges even. Clip into the seam allowance at frequent intervals. Stitch a ½-in seam, and press.

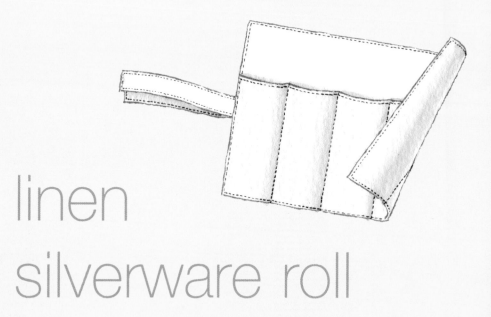

linen
silverware roll

This stylish linen roll is perfect for storing or transporting flatware. Use it for picnics, or store special-occasion knives and forks in it. You can alter the measurements to make it as large or small as you wish—for a picnic you could make individual sleeves for each place setting, and include a pocket for a napkin. The pocket widths can also be adapted—stitch wide ones for spoons and serving implements, and narrower ones for knives and forks.

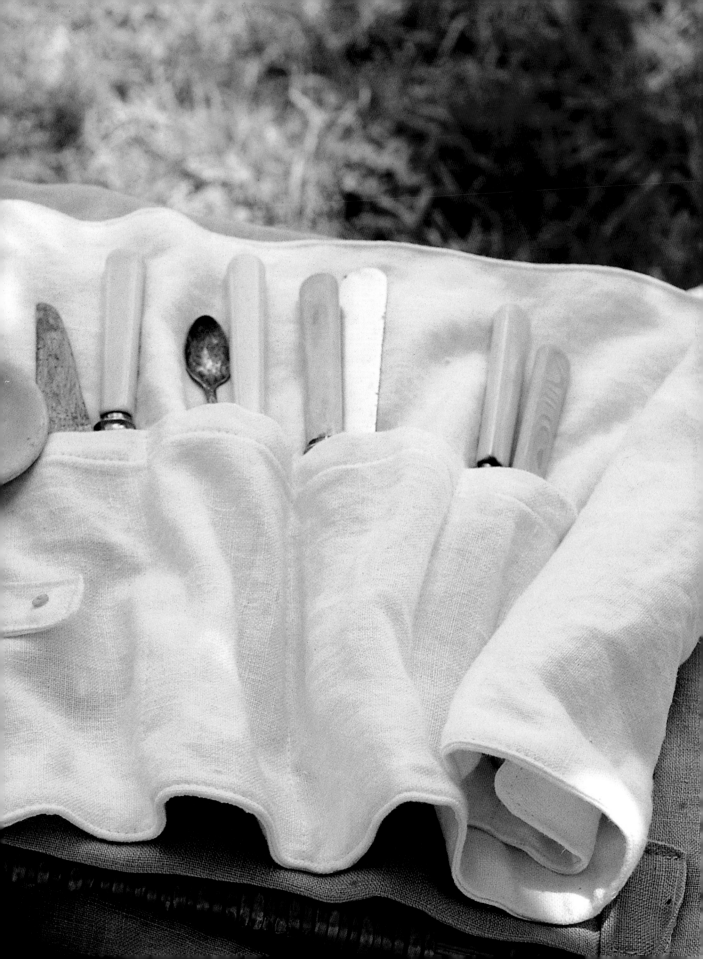

YOU WILL NEED

Yardstick

Scissors

Linen

Pins

Sewing machine and thread

1 Cut a rectangle of linen 20 x 15-in for the backing. Cut a second rectangle 7 x 15-in for the pocket. Fold over, pin, and stitch a ½-in hem along one long edge of the smaller rectangle— this will be the top edge of the pocket.

TIP

If you wish, make the pocket and backing each 4-in deeper, so the backing can be folded over before the linen is rolled up, to safeguard the contents completely.

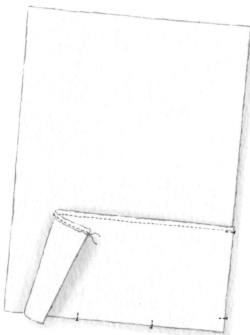

2 Place the smaller rectangle on top of the large rectangle, with its long raw edge matching one of the short raw edges of the large piece and with the hem facing inward. Both pieces should be right side up. Pin, then baste the pocket to the backing piece.

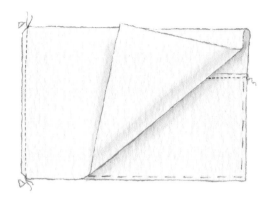

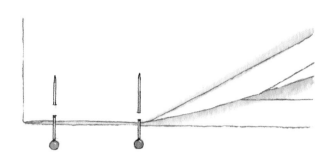

3 Fold the large rectangle in half, so the pocket is enclosed on the inside. Pin the side seams, then stitch a ½-in seam. Trim the corners, remove the basting, then turn right side out. Press.

4 Turn in ½-in along the lower raw edges and pin. Topstitch all around the outer edge of the backing piece.

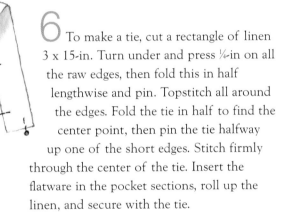

6 To make a tie, cut a rectangle of linen 3 x 15-in. Turn under and press ¼-in on all the raw edges, then fold this in half lengthwise and pin. Topstitch all around the edges. Fold the tie in half to find the center point, then pin the tie halfway up one of the short edges. Stitch firmly through the center of the tie. Insert the flatware in the pocket sections, roll up the linen, and secure with the tie.

5 Decide on the width of the individual pockets and then mark the stitching lines with pins. Stitch along the marked lines, stopping at the top edge of the pocket.

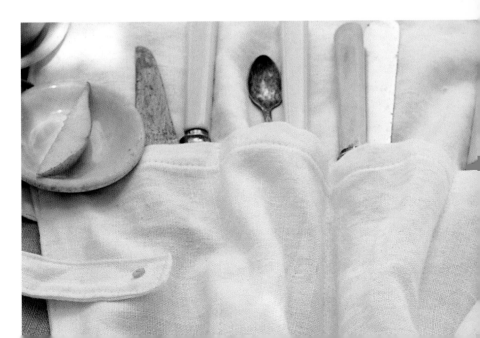

index

author's acknowledgments

Many thanks to Christine Wood for her elegant design and for all her support.
Thank you to Kate Simunek for translating my instructions into such
beautiful artworks. And a big thank you to Cindy Richards,
Alison Wormleighton and Corinne Asghar and all at Cico Books.